THE FULL HOWIE

WRITTEN BY
GARETH K. BENNETT

ILLUSTRATIONS BY
JIM AGPALZA

Published by Rooster Republic Press
Copyright ©2018 Gareth K. Bennett
Art by Jim Agpalza
Edited by Nicholas Day

Visit our catalogue at
www.roosterrepublicpress.com

EXT. JARVIS AND GERRARD - NIGHT

A busy intersection: a Harvey's
Hamburgers, sleazy TAVERN, CHURCH
and CONDO. Four corners, HOOKERS
working each one.

PEDESTRIANS walk aimlessly along
as cars pass. On the far side is
a YOUNG MAN (early 20s, plain)
walking against the tide of
people. His name, we'll learn, is
PHIL.

Phil nervously approaches one of
the street-walkers, a LARGE BLACK
WOMAN with huge HAIR. We can't
hear what they're saying -- only
the SOUND of PASSING CARS. Phil
speaks, gesturing and smiling
pleasantly, suddenly she RAISES
HER HAND indignantly and walks
away -- dccply offended.

Phil lowers his head and
continues along the street to the
next prostitute -- a ROTUND WHITE
WOMAN. Phil speaks to her for

just a moment before she SPITS IN HIS FACE, and struts away on her 8-INCH HEELS.

Poor Phil wipes the SPITTLE off and continues along the strip. The last hooker in line, a MEATY BRUNETTE, wraps a long FEATHER BOA around his neck as they chat. She nods once, twice, and then SLAPS HIM ACROSS THE FACE.

Downcast, Phil walks on, exiting frame.

TITLE: The Full Howie

EXT. HARVEY'S - LATER

Phil sits on a BENCH, crestfallen. We can get a better look at him now: he's your typical, straight-laced, clean-shaven university student. His head in his hands, he looks like he might cry.

          WOMAN (O.S.)

    Why so glum, chum?

Phil looks up.

Another HOOKER is standing beside him, her leg up on the bench giving him a view UP HER SKIRT. She's on the older side of most of the girls on the street, but by far the most beautiful.

This is APPLE (mid-40s, sexy and

wise). She lights a CIGARETTE and looks down on him with a sultry smile.

> APPLE

Name's Apple, like the fruit. And I'm a professional 'frown spinner.'

Apple sits beside him and crosses her legs gracefully.

> APPLE (cont'd)

I'm listening.

Phil looks at her skeptically.

> PHIL

Listen, "Apple." I'm sorry I just don't feel comfortable talking to you.

> APPLE

Really? I'm comfortable with you.

> PHIL

Well, I'm not a hooker am I?

> APPLE

Ouch. Why does it make a lick of difference what I do for a living?

Phil considers this.

APPLE (cont'd)

Come on, I'm a good listener.

PHIL

Okay, I'll bite. My girlfriend and I...

(sighs, this hurts)

EX-GIRLFRIEND now. We broke up a few weeks ago. Been together since grade eight--

APPLE

That's tough. What's her name?

PHIL

You wouldn't *know* her.

APPLE

Please. I want the WHOLE picture.

PHIL

Okay. It was Lilly.

APPLE

And you? What's your handle?

PHIL

(sighs)

I'm Phil.

APPLE

(pondering)

Phil and Lilly--

PHIL

Lilly and Phil.
Everyone used to say
Lilly and Phil.

APPLE

Why'd she break it off?

PHIL

I ended it. She's in
school in Montreal. I
went to surprise her on
her birthday and caught
her...fucking this
guy--

APPLE

Shit! That sucks. Long
distance relationships
can be tough.

Apple slides closer to Phil and
changes her tone -- getting down
to business.

APPLE (cont'd)

What are you doing out
here? There are no long
term girls on Jarvis.

PHIL

I need to get laid.

                    APPLE

        Now we're talking. But
        why pay for it? You're
        a smart looking fella.
        Don't tell me you can't
        get one of those
        college girls to bend
        for a friend.

                    PHIL

        I've had a couple of
        flings, but they didn't
        help. Lilly was...
        special.

Phil is suddenly uncomfortable.

                    APPLE

            (amused)

        Special. I'm sure--

                    PHIL

        You have to understand,
        she and I grew up
        together. We grew, you
        know...sexually.

        (after a beat)

        There was this *thing*
        she did that -- it
        seems -- no one else
        can do.

Apple smiles coyly.

                    APPLE

Uh huh...heard that
before.

PHIL

Really?

APPLE

Happens all the time.
The heart-break Johns.
They're usually older
than you but--

PHIL

I need it bad, Apple.
I'm going crazy. I
can't sleep, I can't
eat and my classes are
suffering.

APPLE

You're looking to turn
your blue balls pink?
That it?

PHIL

It's bigger than that
for me. I can't tell my
folks. I'm so alone.

APPLE

I hear you. So what can
this Apple do for you?

He stares at her, sizing her up.

PHIL

I don't know...a couple

of these... *ladies*, hit
me after I just asked--

          APPLE

Hit you, who?

          PHIL

     (pointing)

Her and her, she spit
on me and that one
there punched me in the
kidney.

          APPLE

     (getting nervous)

What'd you ask them?

          PHIL

If they would do...*the
thing*. The thing only
Lilly did.

          APPLE

     (worried)

What is it?

          PHIL

We called it...birth.

          APPLE

The fuck is *birth*?

Phil leans in and whispers it in
her ear. Her smile fades.

        APPLE (cont'd)

Oh, Christ.

        PHIL

    (tearing up)

It's beautiful. I can
hear her heart beating.
I feel safe, at home.
And after I come...I'm
born again. It's
incredible!

        APPLE

Not a lot of people
looking for that. You
know they're looking
for Handy J's, B-Jobs,
Classic Vag, you name
it. But what you want,
on the street is
called: 'The Full
Howie'.

        PHIL

Full How-ie? Why's it
called that?

        APPLE

You know Howie Mandel,
the comedian? He used
to pull surgical gloves
over his head. A Half-
Howie's up to the nose
but a Full Howie is all
the way in. It's a

                    specialty move. Only a
                    pro can pull it off.
                    Couple of girls died
                    back in the early
                    nineties. Union sent
                    out warnings.

Apple spits on the sidewalk.

                    APPLE (cont'd)

          The Full Howie. Fuck.

Phil puts his head back in his
hands.

                    PHIL

          So, it's hopeless?

Apple looks at him with pity.

                    APPLE

          Listen... Phil...
          I'll...

Phil looks up.

                    APPLE (cont'd)

          I've done it before --
          twice.

Phil smiles.

                    PHIL
               (excited)
          And you'll--
                    APPLE

(getting serious)

But understand, it's a one time only offer. I don't want to see you around here again. Five hundred up front and...I have ground-rules.

PHIL

Whatever you say!

Apple looks around nervously.

APPLE

Let's go.

She grabs his hand and they head down the street.

EXT. WAVERLY HOTEL - ESTABLISHING - NIGHT

A filthy hotel on busy street. HOMELESS MEN shuffle outside like zombies. We hear a SQUELCHING SOUND.

INT. HOTEL ROOM - CONTINUOUS

Apple is GREASING UP PHIL'S HEAD with tons of LUBE.

> APPLE
>
> Now you say you've done this before, that's good. But I have had some...situations in the past and people got hurt. Here are my rules: You have thirty seconds. I'll keep time and when I say, you come out, got it?

> PHIL
>
> Yeah.

> APPLE
>
> I'll knock my knees together like this when time's up.

Phil nods.

> APPLE (cont'd)
>
> Good. I need a second to prepare...

She reaches into her PURSE pulls
out two PINK PILLS and a JOINT.
She pops the pills, lights the
bud and TAKES A HIT.

            APPLE (cont'd)

        (exhaling)

    AHHHH.....you want?

            PHIL

    No, thanks.

            APPLE

    I'll just take a second
    to relax... everything.

She takes another DEEP HIT, holds
it and releases, the room fills
with SWEET SMOKE.

EXT. HARVEY'S - NIGHT

A fidgety, IRRITATED MAN walks up
to the corner and looks around.
He's WHITE, has CORN-ROWS and all
of his visible teeth are GOLD.
His eyes are CRAZY. He wears a
loose fitting TRACK SUIT and GOLD
CHAINS. This is C.H. (28, mean,
insane)

            C.H.

        (to himself)

    Where that bitch?

One of the HOOKERS from across
the street walks past. C.H. grabs

her roughly.

> C.H. (cont'd)
>
> Where's Apple at! You
> seen Apple? Where my
> bitch at?

> HOOKER
>
> I don't know C.H. Last
> I saw she was talking
> to this guy--

> C.H.
>
> They leave together?

> HOOKER
>
> Yeah, jumped in a cab.

> C.H.
>
> Shit.

C.H. jumps into a waiting
SPARKLE-BLUE HONDA CIVIC and
speeds off.

INT. HOTEL ROOM - LATER

Apple takes a last inhale and
puts out the joint in an ASHTRAY.

> APPLE
>
> Okay. I think I'm
> there,. You set?

Phil, dripping with OOZING LUBE,
nods.

                    APPLE (cont'd)

     Good.

Apple removes her PANTIES, gets
on all fours on the BED and hikes
up her SKIRT.

                    APPLE (cont'd)

     Okay, line it up.

Phil gets behind her, she adjusts
him a little.

                    APPLE (cont'd)

     Okay, take a breath and
     when I say go, you
     push. And remember when
     I tap my knees together
     you pull out, okay?

                    PHIL

     Got it. Thank you,
     Apple.

                    APPLE

     Shut up, it's just
     business. Now get in my
     ass.

Apple looks at her watch.

                    APPLE (cont'd)

     Okay...one, two,
     THREE!!!

Phil PUSHES, Apple WINCES, the
sound of STRETCHING, a moment of
hesitation and then 'POP!' --

he's in.

Phil's completely IN Apple -- up to his shoulders. It's The Full Howie, baby!

>PHIL
>
>(in heaven, muffled)

AAHHHHhhh... HHHHHmmmmmm....

Apple's in agony and struggles with her WATCH, she presses START. 30 seconds. The timer begins counting down.

>APPLE
>
>(to herself)
>
>Relax, just relax...

She starts breathing deeply, meditatively.

INT. WAVERLY HOTEL - LOBBY - MOMENTS LATER

The place is filthy and run down. Behind the front desk is a hunched, unshaven DESK CLERK(LATE 50s, hopeless) with a greasy comb-over and sunken eyes.

C.H. rushes in past the maître d' and up the stairs -- he knows where he's going -- been here many times before.

INT. HOTEL ROOM - CONTINUOUS

26 seconds, 25, 24... Apple is

looking more and more relaxed. She is not enjoying herself but she's not suffering anymore.

Phil on the other hand -- or what we can see of him -- is in heaven. Body swooning. MOANS of pleasure.

                    APPLE
                (straining)
        Things you do for
        money, woman... what
        are you going to do
        with your life? You
        can't keep doing this.
        What happened to your
        dream?

INT. WAVERLY HOTEL - HALLWAY - CONTINUOUS

C.H. steps from the elevator and looks around.

                    C.H.
        Apple!! Where are you!!

He starts walking down the hall. Past the doors 301, 302, 303...

INT. HOTEL ROOM - CONTINUOUS

14 seconds, 13, 12, 11...

                    APPLE
        Come on, so close.
        Here...we...

INT. WAVERLY HOTEL - HALLWAY - CONTINUOUS

304! C.H. reaches the door.

> C.H.

Bitch!!

He POUNDS on the door violently!

> C.H. (cont'd)

APPLE!!

INT. HOTEL ROOM - NIGHT

The clock reaches ZERO, Apple looks up in terror!

> C.H. (V.O.)

Where's my money!!

> APPLE

SHIT!

APPLE STANDS SUDDENLY. There is a terrible SLURPING SOUND as Phil is SUCKED UP INSIDE APPLE'S BODY. First his torso, then hips, legs and finally...he's gone.

The door flies open and C.H. rushes in.

Apple looks back to where Phil isn't.

> APPLE (cont'd)

Oh...shit!

C.H.

Bitch, we have a lot to
talk about.

She turns and looks at him, fed
up.

APPLE

And what's that?

C.H.

I don't want no lip
from you.

C.H. looks around.

C.H. (cont'd)

(confused)

You alone?

APPLE

What's it look like?

C.H.

You make my money?

She throws him some CASH. He
counts it and looks at her.

C.H. (cont'd)

(amazed, disappointed)

Good job.

C.H. exits. Apple sits down on
the bed, her head in her hands.

                    APPLE

          Fuck.

INT. ASS - MOMENTS LATER

Phil is face down in MUCK. He
slowly raises his head and looks
around.

Darkness surrounds him, nothing
is clear, only shadows and shapes
in the DARKNESS. There's a
constant HUM, like the sound in
the BELLY OF A SHIP.

                    PHIL

          Where...

There's a sudden movement,
SOMEONE or SOMETHING'S in the
shadows.

                    PHIL (cont'd)

          Hello?

Phil slowly stands and looks
around.

                    PHIL (cont'd)

          Who's there?

Phil reaches into his pocket and
pulls out a PACK OF MATCHES, he
rips one off and goes to strike
it...

                    MAN'S VOICE

          You light that, we both
          die.

                    25

                    PHIL

              (confused)

        What? Why?

              MAN'S VOICE

        Put the God Damn
        matches down and I'll
        answer your question.

                    PHIL

        Okay...

Phil lowers the matches and a MAN
steps out of the shadows.

CLICK! The man turns on a
FLASHLIGHT.

The MAN (50s, grizzled) has a
LONG GRAYING BEARD. He's stoic,
chiseled and has a rustic charm
about him. He resembles a
prospector from the Old West. He
wears a MINER'S HELMET with HEAD
LAMP. This is Ned.

                    NED

        Methane everywhere.
        Match'll blow us up.
        Death by angel.

                    PHIL

        Excuse me?

                    NED

        Follow me. I'll take
        you to my camp.

Ned turns.

        PHIL

What's happening? Where
are we?

        NED

What is the last thing
you remember?

        PHIL

I think I passed out.

        NED

You didn't pass out.
When were you with,
Apple?

        PHIL

Apple?

        NED

Don't play dumb. Apple,
the pretty hooker?

    (he slaps the wet wall)

Her.

        PHIL

Wait, what?

        NED

If you don't know her,
how'd you end up in her
ass?

Phil stops dead.

PHIL

What the hell are you
talking about?

NED

Her asshole, daisy-
chain, her asshole.
We're inside Apple's
ass!

PHIL

Jesus.

NED

He can't help you down
here. No one can.

INT. ASS CAMP - LATER

Phil and Ned sit by a small encampment complete with a SMALL TENT, ADIRONDACK CHAIRS and HOT PLATE masquerading as a fire. Ned heats HOT DOGS over the hot plate.

          PHIL
       (bewildered)
     I don't get it. Any of
     this.

          NED
     Neither do I. If I did,
     maybe I could work on
     getting the hell out.

          PHIL
     There has to be a way.
     We got in
     here...somehow--

          NED
     He never got out.

He points over to a SKELETON on the ground.

          PHIL
     Oh, Christ!

          NED
     He was here when I got

here.

>   PHIL

How *long* have you been
here?

>   NED

Must be going on three
years now. Time seems
to come to a stand
still when you're in
here. No point of
reference.

>   PHIL

This is crazy! There
has to be a way out!

>   NED

Why do people always
have to see things for
themselves? Come here.

INT. ASS - MOMENTS LATER

Phil and Ned stand where the
walls and floor come together. On
the wall is a huge, fleshy
REVERSE ANUS.

>   NED

That's where you came
in. But there's no
getting out. I've tried
everything. Tried
prying her open,
burning her, cutting

her. It's too damn
strong, *she's* too damn
strong.

Phil tries with all his might to
open the anus, but it's no use.
Phil pushes his arm through the
hole but can't get more then his
finger tips through.

Phil turns and looks back.

> PHIL

What's at the *other*
end?

INT. ASS - LATER

The two men stand at a WALL OF
VEINS and another tight SPHINCTER
on the wall -- larger and cleaner
looking then the anus.

> NED

Easier to fit through,
but once you pass
through, there's
nothing but shit. Walls
of excrement that build
up and move through
her. And it pushes you
right along with it.

> PHIL

Could we ride it out of
here?

NED

I've tried. When you
hit the end it scrapes
you right off the
bastard. I even buried
myself into the turds
but it's no use.

PHIL

Fuck.

NED

Don't lose hope--

PHIL

FUCK!!

NED

Calm down, make the
best of it. Accept--

PHIL

FUCK! FUCK! FUCK!!!

Phil runs around slamming his
FISTS against the FLESHY WALLS.
They give a little against the
barrage.

NED

Stop! Stop it!!

PHIL

I want out!!! OUT!!
FUCK!! I'm not going
out LIKE THIS!!

Phil is losing it as he slams the
walls and GOUGES HIS FINGERS into
the FLESH causing the walls to
BLEED.

Ned tackles him.

                    NED

         Don't. I've tried it --
         if you don't stop
         she'll...

There is a DEEP RUMBLING in the
distance. The sound sobers Phil
right up. Both men stare in the
direction of the sound.

                    PHIL

         She'll what?

There is another rumbling, this
time much louder than the first.

                    NED

         Hold on to something,
         anything, just don't
         let go!

                    PHIL

         What will she do?

Suddenly a torrent of WHITE FOAM
pours in.

                    NED

         ANTACID!!!

The two men are WASHED ALONG THE
FLOOR! Somehow, Ned manages to

grab a hold of a ROPE and hold on
to the two of them.

            NED (cont'd)

    HOLD ON!!!

They brace like two men caught in
a flash flood as the FOAM slowly
recedes. They collapse exhausted.

            NED (cont'd)

    Pays to be good to her,
    even in here. If not,
    she can turn on us.

            PHIL

    (winded)

    Okay...okay...

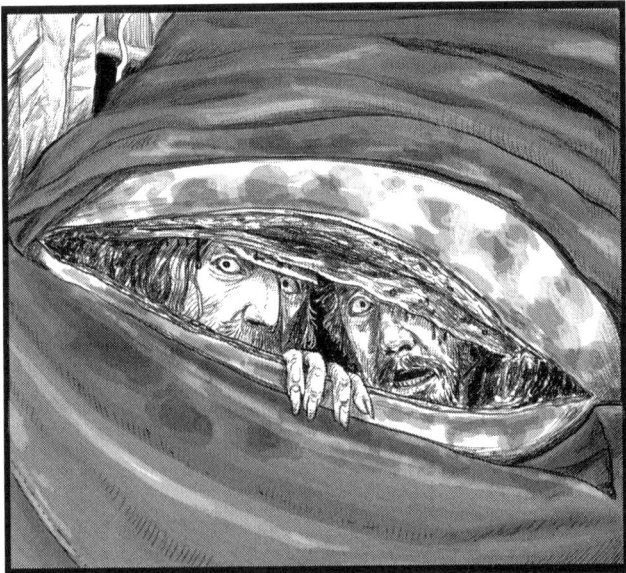

INT. APARTMENT - NIGHT

Apple puts a bottle of TUMS back on the shelf and BURPS loudly.

SIOUXSIE (42, friendly roommate), walks in behind her.

>   SIOUXSIE
>
>   Stomach again?
>
>   APPLE
>
>   It's been fine for the
>   last while but tonight
>   it started acting up
>   again.
>
>   SIOUXSIE
>
>   Why are you home so
>   early?

Apple starts to tear up.

>   APPLE
>
>   I... I lost another
>   one.
>
>   SIOUXSIE
>
>   Oh, fuck. I'm sorry.

Apple breaks down and Siouxsie HOLDS HER.

>   APPLE
>
>   I'm such an idiot. I
>   can't... I'm done. I
>   can't do this anymore,

I'm going straight,
Siouxsie. I have to.

SIOUXSIE

What about C.H.?

APPLE

Fuck him, that little
fuck. I am going away,
I'm going straight
Siouxsie. I'm doing it
this time.

SIOUXSIE

What'll you do?

APPLE

Flowers, maybe. I
always dreamed of
flower arranging. Maybe
this is my chance.

SIOUXSIE

Sounds like you.

That makes Apple want to cry.

APPLE

Thanks, honey.

The two women hug warmly.

INT. ASS - DAY

Phil looks through Ned's stuff.
GLOW STICKS, VISE-GRIPS and a
SPATULA. He holds up a CANDY-
CANE?

                    PHIL

          Where did you get all
          this stuff?

                    NED

          You'd be amazed what
          gets put up a hooker's
          ass.

                    PHIL

          And food, what do we
          eat?

                    NED

          That, my friend, will
          take some getting used
          to.

                    PHIL

          Meaning?

                    NED

          We hunt.

                    PHIL

          Hunt?

INT. ASS - LATER

The two men stand with LARGE
SHARPENED STICKS, waiting like
spear fishermen.

                    PHIL

          How long do we have to
          wait here?

                    NED

        Not long now...

There's a RUMBLING.

                NED (cont'd)

        Get ready! Aim for
        colors, anything with
        color is probably
        edible.

Suddenly a LARGE SHIT, the size
of a subway train, emerges from
the sphincter on the wall and
pushes through the room.

                NED (cont'd)

        Remember, the colors!

Ned throws his spear at the shit
and so does Phil. They both get
HEFTY CHUNKS of what looks like
CORN and ALMONDS.

                    PHIL

            (out of breath)

        How'd we do?

Ned quickly grabs a large MASONRY
JAR and runs behind the exiting
shit.

                    NED

        Not done yet!

The SHIT moves past and exits
through the ANUS. Ned races up
and holds out the JAR.

                    PHIL

          What are you--

There is the loud sound of "Kur-
plop!" and then FRESH WATER flows
from the anus and quickly fills
the jar.

                    NED

          Back-splash. It's
          fresh. Want a sip?

Phil shakes his head in disgust.

                    PHIL

          No...I don't feel so
          good.

                    NED

          You'll get used to it.
          You have to.

Ned take a big drink of the WATER
and wipes his mouth.

                    NED (cont'd)

          God this woman's
          regular. You could set
          your watch by her
          movements.

Phil stares in disbelief.

INT. FLOWER SHOP - DAY

A small but bountiful flower
shop. A LARGE WOMAN (40s,
bookish) stands behind the
counter. She has tight curly hair
and reading glasses low on her
nose.

A CUTE GUY (40s, wise, kind and
no ring) browses.

The door opens with a JINGLE and
Apple steps in, lovely in her

40

civilian clothes, with her hair
pulled back and no make-up, she's
a new woman.

Apple steps up to the counter.
The lady behind the counter
scowls -- she recognizes Apple.

>   APPLE
>
>   Excuse me, miss?

The woman forces a smile.

>   CLERK
>
>   I'm sorry washrooms are
>   for patrons only.

Apple's instantly embarrassed.

>   APPLE
>
>   No...I was wondering if
>   you have any positions
>   available?

>   CLERK
>
>   I don't swing that way
>   sister.

>   APPLE
>
>   Pardon?

>   CLERK
>
>   I don't buy that heart
>   of gold crap! You want
>   a job selling flowers?
>   Look someplace else,
>   'cause I don't hire
>   whores!

41

APPLE

I...I'm...

Mortified, Apple rushes out of
the store.

INT. ASS - DAY

Ned whittles a LARGE SHARP STICK.
There is a DEEP RUMBLING above
them. They look up.

NED

Something's going on up
there. She's not happy.
If this doesn't stop we
could be in for...

(he doesn't even want to say it)

Diarrhea.

PHIL

Jesus! What can we do?

NED

Not much. It's like
weather. You just have
to ride it out.

PHIL

Could we drown?

NED

I've survived dozens of
diarrhea storms. I
reckon I could survive
one more.

PHIL

You know, that's been
bugging me. Why doesn't
it smell worse?
Shouldn't the stink be
unbearable?

NED

There's this old
Russian trick where you
sit in a chair loaded
with dynamite and set
it off. Supposedly
there's a vacuum and
the blast doesn't hurt
you. You're too close
to the explosion to get
hurt. Saw Dennis Hopper
do it once. I figure
you and I are here at
the source of the
smell, at ground zero
of the stink, there
must be a vacuum of
some kind and we don't
really smell it. You
see?

PHIL

Not really.

NED

We're at the epicenter
of the filth and there
is--

43

A massive rumbling above them.

                    NED (cont'd)

     We'd better take cover
     that sounds like a big
     one.

EXT. PARK - DAY

Apple sits on a bench, her face
tear stained, looking miserable.

                    MAN (O.S.)

     Excuse me?

Apple looks up, it's the CUTE GUY
from the flower shop.

                    APPLE

     What?

                    MAN

     I was in Fanny's--

                    APPLE

          (annoyed)
     So what?

                    MAN

     So I came over to tell
     you I told her that
     she's a bitch and I'll
     never shop there again.

                    APPLE

          (taken aback)
     Oh? Thanks.

He holds out a small paper bag.

> MAN

Muffin?

> APPLE

(touched)

You bought me a muffin?

> MAN

Full disclosure, I bought it for myself earlier but you look so sad I thought, if you liked muffins, then it might cheer you up.

Apple smiles.

> APPLE

What kind?

> MAN

Bran.

Apple takes the muffin.

> APPLE

Thanks.·

She starts munching.

> MAN

You're welcome. I'm Adam by the way.

> APPLE

I'm Apple.

She bites the muffin but can't take her eyes off *him*.

INT. ASS - DAY

Ned and Phil have LARGE MASON JARS on their heads and are TIED UP TOGETHER against the wall.

> NED
>
> Sounds like the storm's passing.

> PHIL
>
> (pulling off his "helmet")
>
> Thank god, you had me scared shitless.
> Anymore corn left?

> NED
>
> There's always corn.

INT. RESTAURANT - NIGHT

Apple and Adam sit in a little romantic bistro.

> APPLE
>
> And if you put a penny in the vase it keeps the water fresher, longer.

> ADAM
>
> A penny, really? You do know a lot about flowers.

APPLE

I've loved them since I was a kid, playing in my mother's garden.

ADAM

Why aren't you in flowers now, wait, can you say that, 'in flowers'?

APPLE

(laughing)

I *think* you can. I just lost my way. But I'm getting things together now.

They stare at each other. Adam smiles.

ADAM

I'm glad. I like you. I'd like to see you again, Apple.

APPLE

I think that can be *arranged*.

They both laugh starring deeply into each others' eyes.

INT. APARTMENT - NIGHT

The apartment is dark. The FRONT DOOR swings open and Apple and

Adam enter KISSING PASSIONATELY.

>   ADAM
>
>   (breathlessly)
>
>   Can I come in?
>
>   APPLE
>
>   No, I'm sorry. I need
>   to take this super-
>   slow, okay?
>
>   ADAM
>
>   Definitely. Goodnight,
>   Apple.
>
>   APPLE
>
>   'Night.

Adam exits. Apple closes and
slowly locks the door.

>   APPLE (cont'd)
>
>   (excited)
>
>   Yes, yes, yes!!

Siouxsie, wearing PAJAMAS, steps
into the hall.

>   SIOUXSIE
>
>   I take it you weren't
>   working?
>
>   APPLE
>
>   Fuck that. I'm never
>   working AGAIN!
>
>   (proudly)

48

> No, from now on I'm 'in
> flowers'!

MONTAGE - APPLE TURNS THINGS
AROUND

Set to an UPBEAT POP-SONG à la
"Do You believe in Magic" by The
Lovin' Spoonful or "Break My
Stride" by Mathew Wilder.

-- Apple sits in a packed
classroom as a TEACHER (45,
goatee) talks passionately.
Written on a WHITEBOARD is:

"Small Business Dos and Don'ts".

Apple listens intently,then jots
something down in her NOTEBOOK.

-- Apple and Adam walk along a
busy street HOLDING HANDS. She's
excitedly telling a story, Adam
laughs.

-- Phil has a longer beard now
and entertains Ned with a PUPPET
SHOW using over-sized CORN
KERNELS with faces drawn on.

-- In a floral arranging class,
Apple concentrates as she
ARRANGES blue and white FLOWERS.
A TEACHER (40s, blonde)walks past
and nods with an approving smile.

-- Apple and Adam MAKE LOVE in
her apartment.

-- Apple and her fellow STUDENTS stand at the front of the class under a banner that reads,

"Congrats Grads!"

Everyone cheers! Adam is in the crowd CLAPPING and WHISTLING proudly.

-- Ned concentrates trying to fix an OLD RUSTED FOLDING CHAIR. Suddenly Phil appears, now sporting a SHORT BEARD and RUBS SHIT IN NED'S FACE.

Ned wipes away the FILTH and slowly turns with a BIG SMILE. Ned jumps up and the two engage in a good-natured SHIT-FIGHT!

-- A STRAWBERRY is held under the FLOWING BROWN of a CHOCOLATE FOUNTAIN. Apple and Adam are in a BUFFET RESTAURANT. Adam offers her a bite from the BROWN BERRY.

She goes to take a bite when she notices he's holding a SMALL BLUE BOX -- he opens it revealing a RING! She is in awe.

-- Apple and Adam are being married by a JUSTICE OF THE PEACE (50s, Bob Ross type, white afro). Siouxsie holds a BEAUTIFUL BOUQUET and is trying to hold back tears. Beside her C.H. sits, arms crossed, annoyed. The

Justice finishes and...they're husband and wife! They kiss and everyone applauds!

EXT. FLORAL DESIGNS BY APPLE - DAY

It's Apple's new store! A BANNER above the entrance reads: "Grand Opening!" There's a small CLOSED SIGN in the WINDOW.

Apple and Adam stand proudly in front of the shop.

>ADAM

>> Ready to start your new life?

She nods.

>ADAM (cont'd)

>> Then do it!

Apple runs in and turns the CLOSED SIGN to OPEN!

INT. ASS - DAY

The two men sit quietly. Both their beards, now comically long -- like ZZ Top long.

There's a sound, like a SUBWAY getting closer. They both look up and listen.

>PHIL

What is it?

                NED

    Don't know. Never heard
    it before.

It gets louder and LOUDER. The
men cover their ears!

INT. DOCTOR'S OFFICE - DAY

Apple is in a large EXAMINATION
CHAIR, her stomach exposed and
covered in JELLY. Adam sits
behind her supportively.

A DOCTOR (30s, female) runs an
ULTRASOUND WAND over Apple's
large belly.

                DOCTOR

    And there's your baby.

On the MONITOR is a BABY.

                APPLE

    Oh wow!

                ADAM

    Beauty...

                DOCTOR

    Ladies and gentlemen,
    we have a boy! There's
    his parts, see.

                APPLE

    A boy!

At the bottom of the SCREEN
appears the BLURRED AND BEARDED

FACES of our INTERNAL DUO.

ADAM

(concerned)

Wait...what's that?

DOCTOR

(unsure)

Static.

The Doc removes the wand.

DOCTOR (cont'd)

Want to hear your
baby's heartbeat?

APPLE

Yes, please!

The doc smiles and places a FETAL
DOPPLER against Apple's tummy.
There's a strange sound, like
radio static and the then the
"BUP, BUP, BUP" of Baby's heart.

ADAM

Wow!

APPLE

Oh, Adam.

Suddenly VOICES come from the
SPEAKER.

NED (O.S.)

...three times before.
But never so...

                APPLE

      What?

The doctor shaker her head,
confused.

                DOCTOR

        Never heard that
        before. Here, I'll try
        from this side...

She moves the WAND around when
suddenly...

            PHIL (O.S.)

        ...you think someone's
        fucking her with...

The doctor TURNS OFF the fetal
Doppler.

                DOCTOR

          (embarrassed)
        This also needs to be
        fixed, evidently.

She puts the Doppler away. Apple
and Adam exchange a look, Apple
looks concerned and guilty. Adam
squeezes her hand.

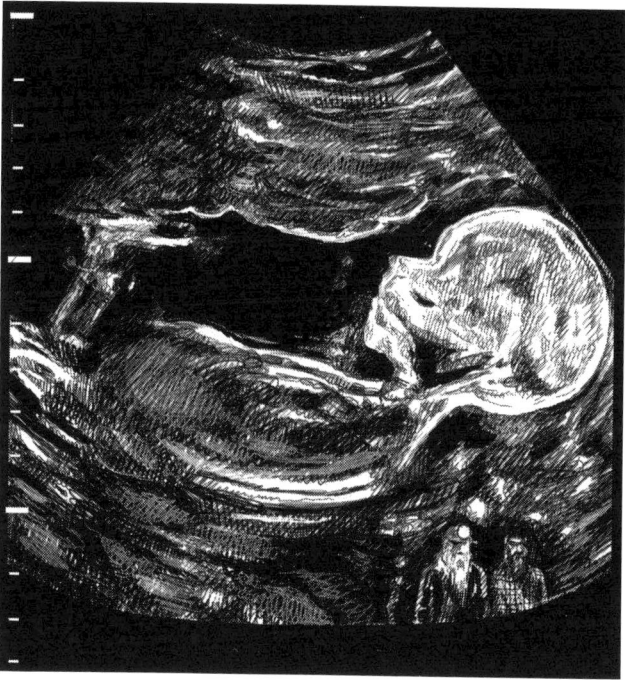

INT. OPERATING ROOM - DAY

Apple is on the OPERATING TABLE.
Adam is beside her holding her
hand. There are three NURSES and
the DOCTOR. A CURTAIN is set up
around her middle so she can't
see the operation.

        APPLE

  This is all a dream,
  isn't it?

        ADAM

  Feels like it--

DOCTOR

Here we go!

ADAM

(seeing the baby)

Oh, wow!!

APPLE

Please, let me see!

DOCTOR

Of course, of course...

The doctor moves a LARGE MIRROR so Apple can see the baby being born.

The doctor raises the INFANT up and into the air.

DOCTOR (cont'd)

It's a boy, alright!

APPLE

(ecstatic)

A boy! A baby boy! Adam a boy!! Can I hold him?

The doctor hands the BABY to Apple.

DOCTOR

You can hold him just for a second. Then we'll patch you -- OH MY GOD!!

Apple looks up at the MIRROR and
sees in the reflection of her
open stomach: NED AND PHIL
STARING OUT of her. With their
BEARDS and TORN CLOTHES they look
like castaways.

One nurses SCREAMS, the Doctor
steps back in awe and Adam FAINTS
to the floor.

The boys make their move:
CLIMBING UP AND OUT of Apple and
into the operating room.

                NED

        (to Apple)

    Sorry, Darlin'

        (to a nurse)

    Excuse us.

                PHIL

    Congratulations!

They RUN OUT OF THE ROOM.

Apple smiles widely, with great
relief.

                APPLE

    It's okay! I know them.

TNT. DINING ROOM - EVENING

CLOSING CREDITS OVER:

APPLE, ADAM and BABY in her
HIGHCHAIR, sit at a TABLE eating

happily.

The camera rests on a LAZY-SUSAN, rotating around the table revealing that PHIL and NED are sitting with them -- now clean-shaven.

Everyone LAUGHING and TALKING, enjoying their supper. A new and unique family having dinner together.

The table is laid with plenty of FOOD, beautiful FLOWERS, and of course -- CORN.

THE END

41493933R00035